TOLES Legal English:

Advanced English for Lawyers, Plain & Simple. International Legal English for Lawyers, Law Professionals & Law Students

(TOLES Edition)

Marc Roche

This is the TOLES Edition of the book
Master Legal Vocabulary & Legal Terminology. It
includes extra chapters for TOLES exam
preparation.

www.idmbusinessenglish.com

Copyright © 2019 **Marc Roche**

Copyright 2019 Marc Roche

IDM Business & Law

www.idmbusinessenglish.com

Contents

About This Book...1
English as the Language of International Business and Law...3
The Challenge...5
Chapter 1: Basic Legal Terms...8
Chapter 2: Key Principles of Contracts & Contract Law...28
Chapter 3: Specific Terms and Language in Contracts...54
Chapter 4: Prepositions in Legal English...72
Chapter 5: Legal English Phrasal Verbs Mini-dictionary with Practice Exercises...86
Chapter 6. Communicating Clearly: Active VS Passive...102
    Active Voice...103
    Passive Voice...106
    How to Avoid Conflict & Be Diplomatic...109
    Converting from Passive to Active Voice...114
Chapter 7. Language & Punctuation Rules...119
    Possessives & Apostrophes...120
    Lists...121
    Business Names...123
    Adding Information with Parenthetical Expressions...123
    Days and Dates...124
    Non-restrictive Relative Clauses...126
    Dependent Clauses...128

Independent Clauses...130
Participial Phrases...131
Avoid Loose Sentences...133
Similar Meaning and Function Should Have a
Similar Form...135
Parentheses...139
Quotations...140
Chapter 8. Word Order...143
Chapter 9. How to Summarize Information...153
Chapter 10. Subject-Verb Agreement...156
Collective Nouns...157
Mixture of Singular and Plural Nouns...163
Sentences with Two Subjects...164
Chapter 11. Verbs Versus Nouns...165
Chapter 12. Ending a Sentence with a
Preposition...168
The Problem with Obsessing Over the Preposition
Guideline...170
Chapter 13. "That" & "Which"...171
Chapter 14. Conjunctions...173
Chapter 15. Ambiguous & Misused Modifiers...179
Case Study: The Rule of the Last Antecedent...180
Lockhart v. U.S....181

Adding Descriptive Information with -ing
phrases...185
Legal Terms Glossary...188
425 Legal Documents and Templates...189
About the Author...190

About This Book

TOLES Legal English: Advanced English for Lawyers, Plain & Simple, provides a structured framework under which law students, lawyers and other law professionals can significantly improve their knowledge of legal vocabulary and terminology for the TOLES test, at both the Higher and Advanced levels.

You will be taken through the main vocabulary and grammar structures in commercial contracts and allowed to practice them through highly targeted vocabulary and grammar activities, which aim to develop, not only your lexical and grammatical skills, but also your confidence and overall competence within international legal settings.

Towards the end of the book you will find a short glossary with all the main terms of contract law and legal vocabulary in English, together with a phrasal verb mini-dictionary which includes definitions and exercises to perfect your mastery of this area of English.

Finally, the last section of this book, contains an amazing selection of 425 legal templates to guide you through drafting contracts, letters, affidavits and many other documents. It will be an invaluable resource for your studies and career in the legal arena.

English as the Language of International Business and Law

Master Legal Vocabulary & Legal Terminology TOLES Edition

There are currently huge differences in the level of importance given to global languages as opposed to local languages. In fact, in the Western world we have seen how, English has gradually been introduced as the lingua franca in both the world of leisure and the world of work. Even areas such as the law, which up until recently remained unaffected by this global shift, are now rapidly changing in their approach to both education and professional development.

In total, there are 320 different jurisdictions worldwide, which can be grouped into three systems, the Anglo-American Common Law group, the Napoleonic group and the Germanic group; However, there are other systems which are growing strongly, such as Islamic law among others.

Non-native English-speaking lawyers are getting used to finding contracts and many other documents in English. In addition, to add more complexity to the issue, the English that Anglo-Saxon system lawyers use in their writing has little to do with what most non-native lawyers learned at school.

The Challenge

In the following chapters we give you some keys to help you improve your understanding of legal vocabulary, terminology and grammar.

Legal English is the language used by lawyers trained in the Anglo-Saxon system. It is a "specialized language", that is, a subset of the language used by a certain group of professionals, in this case, lawyers of the English-speaking countries.

As a specialized language, it has certain characteristics that make it difficult and obscure, even for those who master the concepts in their own language and who have a high level of general English. Recognizing and overcoming these difficulties is essential in order to understand a legal document written in English.

These are, arguably, some of the main difficulties: -

1. Writing style -

2. Use of archaic words -

1. The style of writing

The way in which the Anglo-Saxon jurists write their texts and the style they use in them are quite different to how it is done in other systems.

The clauses of the contracts, for example, usually contain very long sentences, full of subordinate sentences that can make reading difficult.

Sometimes we find clauses of 15 lines in the same sentence. They are so long that one does not know when they end. Unravelling its meaning requires a great effort of concentration. Although, as is logical, there are some tricks that can help us.

The use of capital letters in some words is another characteristic of this particular style. This custom, however, is not a whim, but responds to a very specific purpose: that of identifying certain terms of special relevance in the contract.

2. Use of archaic words "archaisms",

which is how we call these words and old expressions, are very abundant in the Anglo-Saxon contracts and in many other documents.

Some typical examples are words like **hereby, thereto, whereas,** or expressions like **master** and **servant** and **provided that** ... These expressions are not usually used in spoken English even in legal settings, but they survive in written language as magical formulas of legal English that nobody dares to change.

Chapter 1: Basic Legal Terms

The law is a system of rules that people are supposed to follow in a society or country. The courts and police enforce this system of rules and punish people who break the laws such as by making them pay a fine or through another penalty like sending them to jail.

Combinations with the word "Law"

Let's look at some common word partnerships containing the word "law". The word "law" can be combined with an adjective. For example, "civil law" and "criminal law" which we'll look at next. It can be combined with a verb as in "break the law" or "commit a crime". Other examples of this are "enforce the law", meaning to make sure the law is not broken, or "become law" and "pass a law", which are used to refer to when a new law is created by a government.

Areas of Law

<u>Civil Law</u>

Civil law is the part of law that deals with disagreements between private individuals rather than crimes. In many countries, civil laws come from two different sources.

1. Legislation

These are laws created by the government of a country

2. Common Law

These are laws that have been introduced over a long period of time and are based on previous legal decisions.

Civil law is also influenced by local traditions, religious beliefs and culture.

Criminal Law

Criminal law is a system of law concerned with crimes and the punishment of criminals. Criminals are people who commit crimes. Most criminal law is based on government legislation.

Contract Law

Contract law sets rules and agreements to buy and sell items (goods) and services.

Property law

Property law states the rights and obligations that a person has when they buy, sell or rent homes and buildings.

Trust law

Trust law sets out the rules for money that is put into an investment such as pension funds that people save up for their retirement.

TORT Law or Law of TORTS

Tort law helps people to make claims for compensation when someone hurts them or damages their property.

Constitutional Law

Constitutional law is used to create laws on how different levels of governments can act and on human rights.

Administrative Law

Administrative law is used by ordinary citizens who want to challenge decisions made by governments.

International Law

International law is used to set out the rules on how countries can act in areas such as trade, the environment or military action.

The Geneva Conventions on the conduct of war are an example of international law. If people have a problem with the law or they need to take legal action against an individual or a company, they will usually need the help of a lawyer.

Types of Lawyer

A lawyer is someone who has studied law and has a special qualification to represent people in court or in other legal actions.

There are many different types of lawyer and they have different names in British and American English. Here are some of the common ones.

Attorney; this is the word Americans use to describe a lawyer and in British English, we usually call them a solicitor.

If the lawyer is appearing in court, they are called a council in the US and a barrister in the UK. You can tell if a lawyer is a barrister because they wear a traditional costume of a black gown and a white curly wig as you can see in the pictures.

In criminal law, a lawyer either represents the defense or the prosecution. The defense is the lawyer that is defending against the case by trying to prove that the defendant is not guilty of the charges.

The prosecution is the lawyer who represents the government side and is seeking to prove that the defendant is guilty.

A case is a situation that involves a particular person or thing. In the context of today's topic, a case is a legal action that will be decided in a court of law. It is also used to describe the facts that support one side of an argument or a legal dispute.

Collocations with "Case"

Collocations with "case" related to the law include a court case, a criminal case, and a civil case. We can bring a case against somebody, defend a case, the court will consider a case or hear a case. A lawyer can handle a case or prosecute the case. At the end of the court case, we might dismiss the case, settle the case or drop the case and that closes this case.

Types of Law

As mentioned previously, the word 'law' refers generally to legal documents which specify the rules around a particular kind of activity.

Exercise 1: Types of Law

Read the following short texts, which each contain a word used to talk about types of laws. In which kind of document do you think each appeared? Match each text (1-5) with its source (a-e).

Some Vocabulary for this exercise:

Plain meaning rule- this principle means that wherever possible, the most common and obvious meaning of a word should be used and therefore interpreted. This is adhered to as long as it doesn't lead to absurd interpretations within the context.

Ordinance- a law introduced by a local government.

Directive- official guide or instructions

1. The purpose of this directive is to inform military members of national contingents, military observers and civilian police officers of the United Nations policy and procedures on violent conduct. (Source: https://police.un.org/en/directive-sexual-harassment-united-nations-peacekeeping-and-other-field-missions-military-members-of)

Newspaper article

government document

court ruling

2. According to the *plain meaning rule,* if a statute is unambiguous and clear, the literal meaning of the words will apply, so long as that interpretation does not lead to an absurd result.

newspaper

parliamentary speech

court ruling

3. The purpose of this ordinance is to restrict drunk and disorderly behavior on the streets of Manchester for the good of the public.

parliamentary speech

brochure for employees

local government document

4. The Personal Protective Equipment at Work Regulations are designed to prevent personal injuries and illnesses from occurring in the workplace.

court ruling

parliamentary speech

brochure for employees

5. I am pleased to have the opportunity to present the Juvenile Justice Amendment Bill to the House Mr. Speaker. It is a significant step towards the achievement of a fairer more orderly society.

parliamentary speech

newspaper

local government document

Exercise 1 Answers:

1B, 2C, 3C, 4C, 5A

Exercise 2: Types of Law

Match the words below to their definitions.

Bill/ Regulations/ Ordinance/ Amendment/ Statute / Directive

1. Rules issued by a government agency to maintain the principles of a law

2. Law or rule introduced by a town, city or county:

3. Legal draft before being passed as a law:
....

4. Official or formal guidelines or advice :
....

5. Formal written law introduced by a legislative body: ....

Exercise 2 Answers:

1. regulations

2. ordinance

3. bill

4. directive

5. statute

Useful language: Explaining the Law

Stating what the law says in formal settings:

When writing a formal letter or email and summarizing the provisions of a law in English, do not say:

The statute discusses…

The law is about…

The law says…..

The regulation talks about…

You should use one of these structures:

(Please note that this type of language is not always appropriate for explaining the law to clients)

The law …

Provides that

Stipulates that

Sets forth

Governs

Regulates

There are several ways to refer to what a law says.

The law stipulates that companies must have a memorandum of association and articles of association*.

* The memorandum of association is the document that officially sets up the company whereas the articles of association establish how the company is managed, governed and owned.

The law provides that the penalty for a first offence is €200.

The law specifies that the ISA operates both as police and as a national security agency.

The following verbs can also be used to describe or explain what the law says:

The law prescribes that /sets forth / determines / states / lays down

Exercise 1: Types of Court

Match each of the following types of court with the explanation of what happens there (a-i).

magistrates' court

tribunal

crown court

supreme court/ high court

lower court

moot court

small-claims court

appellate court / court of appeals / appeals court

juvenile court

A type of court where minors (people under 18) are tried is called a

....

The court where a case is heard first and whose decisions are subject to review or to appeal to a higher court is called

....

UK court where small crimes are tried is called ....

A court where students of law can practice arguing hypothetical cases in order to practice is called a ....

A court where cases which have already been heard in a lower court are reviewed is called

....

A type of court where cases involving a small amount of money are heard is called

....

A court where cases which involve serious crimes are heard by a judge and a jury in the Britain is called ....

A court where a group of specially chosen people study specific legal issues, such as immigration is called ....

This type of court serves as a last option and is called .... *(usually the highest court in a jurisdiction).

Exercise 1: Answers

a) A type of court where minors (people under 18) are tried is called a juvenile court

b) The court where a case is heard first and whose decisions are subject to review or to appeal to a higher court is called the lower court.

c) A UK court where small crimes are tried is called the magistrates' court.

d) A court where students of law can argue hypothetical cases in order to practice is called a moot court.

e) A court where cases which have already been heard in a lower court are reviewed is called the appellate court.

f) A type of court where cases involving a small amount of money are heard is called the Small-claims court.

g) A court where cases which involve serious crimes are heard by a judge and a jury in the Britain is called the crown court.

h) A court where a group of specially chosen people study specific legal issues, such as immigration is called a tribunal.

Types of tribunal include: Employment tribunals, Immigration Services Tribunal,

Lands Tribunal, Social Security & Child Support Commissioners, The Criminal Injuries and Compensation Appeals Panel, The Mental Health Review Tribunal, Pensions Appeal Tribunals and Asylum & Immigration Tribunal.

i) This type of court serves as a last option and is called the high court.

Chapter 2: Key Principles of Contracts & Contract Law

In this chapter, we'll look at the key principles behind contracts and contract law. If you've ever signed up for broadband internet, booked a trip or bought a phone, you've entered into a contract. There main steps to formalizing a contract are, the intent to make one, an offer, and consideration for both sides.

Basic requirements for a contract to be legally binding:

First, the parties must have made truthful representations in the course of their negotiations. Then, the parties agree on the specifics of the contract and they accept.

Truthful representations during negotiations

Agree specific details

Accept

Legally binding contract is formed

Problems in a Contract

Repudiation

A contract may be threatened when one party does not fulfil its obligations, which can lead to repudiation.

Frustration

When a contract cannot be fulfilled for unforeseen reasons, the legal term is frustration.

Arbitration

When two parties in a contract can't agree, they may try to solve their dispute through a process of arbitration. Arbitration, is when an external person or organization is asked to step in and help solve an issue.

Damages/Compensation

If this doesn't work, one party can try to sue the other in court to be awarded damages or compensation in the case of a breach of contract.

Chapter 2: Exercise 1

Match the words to the definitions. You can check your answers on the next page after the exercise.

Intent

Acceptance

Impracticability

Frustration

Offer; to make or extend an offer

Party; parties to a contract

Contract- to make or form a contract.

Consideration

Damages, to award damages

Arbitration; to arbitrate

To settle a dispute

Repudiation

Representation. to make a representation

Counteroffer

...................⟫⟫ any formal agreement between people or businesses. We are creating a legal relationship.

...................⟫⟫ means that you actually want to create a contract. Without this on both sides, there can be no contract.

...................⟫⟫ when you propose a possible contract to a person or business. It can be accepted, rejected or amended and sent back as a ⟫⟫ ....

...................⟫⟫ something of value however small for both sides.

...................⟫⟫ when both sides agree on a contract. Once this is done, the agreement becomes legal.

.... »» those who are agreeing to do something. It can be a person, a group of people, a business or another type of organization who enters into negotiations or into an agreement.

.... »» Anytime a party makes a statement of fact in a contract or in negotiating a contract.

.... »» When one party does not keep to what was agreed in a contract. This may have consequences outlined in the contract or it may lead to a lawsuit in some cases.

.... »» when the contract cannot be fulfilled due to no fault from either party.

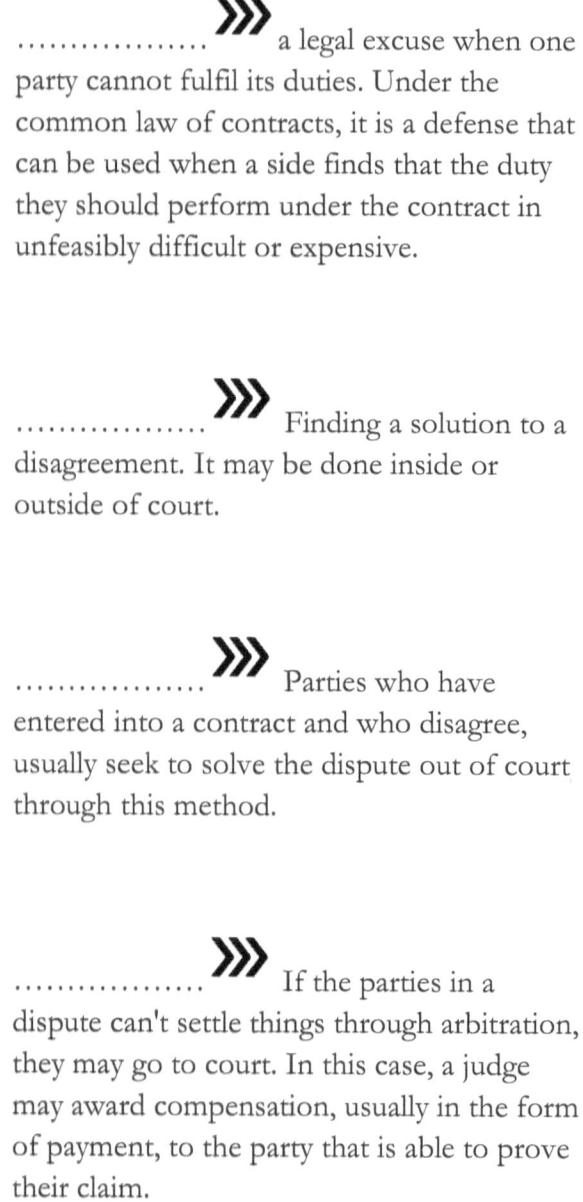

.... a legal excuse when one party cannot fulfil its duties. Under the common law of contracts, it is a defense that can be used when a side finds that the duty they should perform under the contract in unfeasibly difficult or expensive.

.... Finding a solution to a disagreement. It may be done inside or outside of court.

.... Parties who have entered into a contract and who disagree, usually seek to solve the dispute out of court through this method.

.... If the parties in a dispute can't settle things through arbitration, they may go to court. In this case, a judge may award compensation, usually in the form of payment, to the party that is able to prove their claim.

Answers

Contract- to make, create, enter into, sign or form a contract.

Any formal agreement between people or businesses. It creates a legal relationship.

Intent

Means that you actually want to create a contract. Without this on both sides, there can be no contract.

While Anna wanted to make a deal, Jeremy had no intent.

Offer; to make an offer

When you propose a possible contract to a person or business. It can be accepted, rejected or amended and sent back as a **counteroffer.**

Mr. Jone's lawyers sent the offer to the company's legal team.

Consideration

Something of value however small for both sides.

Adam felt that the deal didn't include enough consideration for his party.

Acceptance

When both sides agree on a contract. Once this is done, the agreement becomes legal.

Acceptance of the contract depends on certain facts being verified

Party; parties to a contract

Those who are agreeing to do something. It can be a person, a group of people, a business or another type of organization who enters into negotiations or into an agreement.

Since the two parties couldn't agree, they failed to finalize a deal.

Representation. to make a representation

Anytime a party makes a statement of fact in a contract or in negotiating a contract.

The judge decided that Rola Cola PLC's representations were truthful and accurate.

Repudiation

When one party does not keep to what was agreed in a contract. This may have consequences outlined in the contract or it may lead to a lawsuit in some cases.

Repeated failure to deliver on time led to repudiation of the contract.

Frustration

When the contract cannot be fulfilled due to no fault from either party.

The contract was found to violate trade agreements, which brought about its Frustration.

Impracticability

A legal defense under the common law of contracts when a side finds that the duty they should perform under the contract is unfeasibly difficult or costly.

Bell Ltd. claimed they could not carry out their duties under the contract on the grounds of impracticability.

To settle a dispute

To find a solution to a disagreement. It may be done inside or outside of court.

It took Spain and Italy years to settle their dispute over olive oil branding.

Arbitration; to arbitrate

Parties who have entered into a contract and who disagree, usually seek to solve the dispute out of court through this method.

In an effort to avoid a costly legal battle, the two companies agreed to arbitration.

Damages, to award damages

If the parties in a dispute can't settle things through arbitration, they may go to court. In this case, a judge may award compensation, usually in the form of payment, to the party that is able to prove their claim.

The judge ruled in favor of the complainant and awarded substantial damages.

Chapter 2: Exercise 2:

Read the following sentences. For questions 1-5, write the word which best fits in each space. Use only one word in each space. (You can find the answers underneath this exercise)

GLQ wanted to settle the .... out of court to save on legal fees.

The buyer decided to refuse the .... based on the price.

A contract becomes legal immediately after ....

They celebrated when the judge decided to award them ....

Impracticability and frustration are suitable options for adjusting the relationship between the .... under their agreement when there is poor prediction and the contract cannot be fulfilled.

Answers:

GLQ wanted to settle the dispute out of court to save on legal fees.

The buyer decided to refuse the offer based on the price.

A contract becomes legal immediately after acceptance.

They celebrated when the judge decided to award them damages.

Impracticability and frustration are suitable options for adjusting the relationship between the parties under their agreement when there is poor prediction and the contract cannot be fulfilled.

Offer & Acceptance

Often, particularly when the parties are in contact with each other, they must, by law come to an agreement following acceptance of an offer; however, some situations are not so clear.

Offers can be made to individuals, members of a group, or even the public at large. In order to accept an offer, the one who receives the offer (offeree) must be aware of the existence of said offer. Acceptance can only be made by an intended offeree, and a 'bilateral contract' can never be accepted by silence. Nevertheless, an agreement can sometimes be binding if the offeree shows acceptance by conduct. Acceptance by conduct is where a person or party`s actions indicate implied acceptance of an offer.

Note: Bilateral contracts are those which involve reciprocal obligations. These are the most common type of contract in most cases.

Offers need to be differentiated from an 'invitation to treat'. An invitation to treat is an opportunity to further deal and negotiate, but not an indication that the relevant party's goods or services are available for immediate acceptance.

Products on display in shops and most adverts for goods or services are viewed as mere 'invitations to treat' and are therefore not available to be immediately accepted. An offeree is entitled to make a counter-offer; if this is rejected, and the original offer is not reinstated, the offeree can't go back and accept the initial offer.

Andrews, N. (2011).

Chapter 2: Exercise 3:

Read the adapted text below and think of the word which best fits each space. Use only one word in each space. There is an example at the beginning (*).

An offer may be defined as an indication by one person that he or she is prepared to contract with one or more others, on certain (*) TERMS which are fixed, or capable of being fixed when the offer is made. Distinction should be made between an offer and an invitation to (1) …….. Sometimes one of the parties will simply wish to open negotiations, rather than make an offer that will lead immediately to a contract upon acceptance. For example, in the (2) ………..of Fisher v Bell (1961) it was (3) ………..by the court that goods offered for sale in a shop window with a price attached were not offers according to the law of contract and that a shopkeeper is not (4) ………..by any price displayed. He or she is entitled to say to the customer "that is a mistake". The same principle applies when potential contractors are invited, (for example, by the city council who want to build a new library) to submit quotations to do a specific job at a specific price. According to the law of contract, an invitation to (5) …….. that leads to several interested parties "bidding" for the same contract will not be seen as an offer capable of being accepted but merely as part of the negotiating process.

Even if an offer takes a legally binding form it can still be (6) ……….. in other words "taken back" at any point before it is accepted. The communication of this decision need not necessarily come from the offeror. Provided that the (7) ……… is fully aware at the time that he or she decides to accept the offer that it is no longer open in the mind of the offeror then no acceptance will be possible. An offer may also become incapable of acceptance because of (8)………of time. If the offeror has specified a time in which acceptance must be received, any acceptance outside the time limit cannot create a contract.

There must also be certainty in offer and acceptance. Even though the parties may have appeared to make an agreement by exchange of a matching offer and acceptance, the courts may refuse to (9) ……. it if there appears to be some uncertainty about what has been agreed or if some important aspect of the agreement has been left (10) …….. to be decided later.

(Source: adapted from Law Teacher Net)

Answers:

An offer may be defined as an indication by one person that he or she is prepared to contract with one or more others, on certain (*) TERMS which are fixed, or capable of being fixed when the offer is made. Distinction should be made between an offer and an invitation to (1) treat Sometimes one of the parties will simply wish to open negotiations, rather than make an offer that will lead immediately to a contract upon acceptance. For example, in the (2) ease of Fisher v Bell (1961) it was (3) held by the court that goods offered for sale in a shop window with a price attached were not offers according to the law of contract and that a shopkeeper is not (4) bound by any price displayed. He or she is entitled to say to the customer "that is a mistake". The same principle applies when potential contractors are invited, (for example, by the city council who want to build a new library) to submit quotations to do a specific job at a specific price. According to the law of contract, an invitation to (5) tender that leads to several interested parties "bidding" for the same contract will not be seen as an offer capable of being accepted but merely as part of the negotiating process.

Even if an offer takes a legally binding form it can still be (6) revoked in other words "taken back" at any point before it is accepted. The communication of this decision need not necessarily come from the offeror. Provided that the (7) offeree is fully aware at the time that he or she decides to accept the offer that it is no longer open in the mind of the offeror then no acceptance will be possible. An offer may also become incapable of acceptance because of (8) lapse of time. If the offeror has specified a time in which acceptance must be received, any acceptance outside the time limit cannot create a contract.

There must also be certainty in offer and acceptance. Even though the parties may have appeared to make an agreement by exchange of a matching offer and acceptance, the courts may refuse to (9) enforce it if there appears to be some uncertainty about what has been agreed or if some important aspect of the agreement has been left (10) open to be decided later.

Capacity in Contract Law

Read the following extract about contracts. Choose the best word to fill each gap from A, B, C or D below. For each question 1–6, choose one word (A, B, C or D). There is an example at the beginning (0).

Despite the fact that people vary greatly in how able they are to represent their interests in bargaining processes, an individual is usually (0) assumed to possess the power to enter into a contract. Only in extenuating (1) .... is a person's ability to enter a contract viewed as impaired by law because of her incapacity to fully take part in the bargaining process before the contract is created. An individual whose power is impaired to this degree is regarded as lacking the capacity to form a contract and is (2) .... to a special set of rules which enable her to avoid the contracts that she enters so as to protect her from her own actions. Both mental infirmity and immaturity are (3) .... as impairing the power to contract. However, in the past, marriage, was considered under common law to (4) .... women of their separate legal identities, which included their capacity to

enter into legally binding contracts during
their husband's lifetime. (5) ...., this
perception of disability was almost completely
removed by new statutes which were (6)
.... in the 19th century.

1.

stages

junctures

occasions

circumstances

2.

Liable

Conditional

Subject

Open

3.

Recognized

Conceded

Granted

Appreciated

4.

Dissolve

Debar

Deprive

Dismiss

5.

For example

Consequently

However

Nevertheless

6.

Legislated

Realized

Enacted

Ruled

Answers:

Despite the fact that people vary greatly in how able they are to represent their interests in bargaining processes, an individual is usually (0) assumed to possess the power to enter into a contract. Only in extenuating (1) circumstances is a person's ability to enter a contract viewed as impaired by law because of her incapacity to fully take part in the bargaining process before the contract is created. An individual whose power is impaired to this degree is regarded as lacking the capacity to form a contract and is (2) subject to a special set of rules which enable her to avoid the contracts that she enters so as to protect her from her own actions. Both mental infirmity and immaturity are (3) recognized as impairing the power to contract. However, in the past, marriage, (4) was considered under common law to deprive women of their separate legal identities, which included their capacity to enter into legally binding contracts during their husband's lifetime. (5) Nevertheless, this perception of disability was almost completely removed by new statutes which were (6) enacted in the 19th century.

Chapter 2: Exercise 5

Read the following definitions and then introduce the appropriate term into each gap in the example sentences.

You can check your answers on the next page after the exercise.

Terms, to come to terms.

The terms of a written contract are the specific details that the parties are agreeing to. When parties come to terms, they are reaching agreement on all of these points.

Ratify, to ratify an agreement.

When the parties agree to a contract, they must ratify the agreement. This normally means officially accepting the contract by signing a paper version of it.

Without Prejudice

Sometimes, parties will state or write things in a negotiation, but they do not want these statements to be part of the agreement. These statements can't be used as evidence in legal cases if they are made without prejudice.

Legally binding

If a contract is legally binding, it is valid under the law. The parties are legally tied to the contract and must abide by it.

Example Sentences:

The director issued that particular statement ...., so it cannot not be used in court.

The contract is not ....
because it wasn't signed by the other party.

Following five days of negotiations, they finally .... on a deal.

The signatures of both parties are required in order to ....

Answers:

The director issued that particular statement without prejudice, so it cannot not be used in court.

The contract is not legally binding because it wasn't signed by the other party.

Following five days of negotiations, they finally came to terms on a deal.

The signatures of both parties are required in order to ratify an agreement.

Chapter 3: Specific Terms and Language in Contracts

In the last chapter, we looked at some of the basic principles of contracts. Here, we'll focus on specific terms and language found in contracts.

3.1 Specific Terms: Introduction

Express terms are the specific terms written into the contract or discussed during negotiations.

Implied terms that are not specified directly but still govern the contract.

Conditions are the most important terms of a contract. If a condition is not met, the contract is broken or breached.

The conditions and warranties of a contract are written in **clauses**.

Finally, **boilerplate clauses** are usually included at the end of a contract. They're sometimes called **"miscellaneous" clauses**.

Legal responsibility or liability is spelled out very clearly in the contract. There are three main types of liability.

Joint liability in a contract means that all parties are responsible for the full debt or investment connected to the contract.

Several liability, or limited liability, means that each side is only responsible for their own share of debt or investment.

Joint and several liability (joint and severally liable), means that if an amount is owed, a claimant can demand the full amount from all parties as if they were jointly responsible. The parties then have to agree among themselves how much each one of them has to pay.

Limited liability;

If one party in a contract is a limited company, then that company's owners have limited liability. This means that the owners' assets are protected in case of unpaid debt, lawsuits or bankruptcy for example.

Contracts often have **exclusion clauses** to protect a party legally in certain circumstances.

Warranties are assurances between parties that confirm the accuracy of the facts expressed in the contract.

Now let's look at the vocabulary in more detail with some definitions and examples.

Chapter 3: Exercise 1:

Read the following sentences. For questions 1-5, write the word which best fits in each space. Use only one word in each space. (You can find the answers underneath this exercise)

For example:

We refused to ratify the .... without our solicitors present.

Answer: *We refused to ratify the agreement without our solicitors present.*

1. With so many express ...., the contract was 42 pages long.

2. The contractors and the suppliers were .... and .... liable under the contract.

3. Breaking a .... doesn't necessarily mean the contract is void.

4. The campaign guidelines and schedule were set in accordance with the .... terms of the contract.

5. The lawyer worded the .... of the contract very carefully.

6. Most commercial contracts have a great number of "miscellaneous" clauses towards the back, which are often referred to as ....

7. We read each and every .... of the sale of goods contract very carefully.

8. .... was found to rest with the supplier because they failed to deliver the goods on time due to a series of errors in the supply chain.

9. The company enjoyed ...., so its directors' assets were protected.

10. They asked their lawyer to insert several .... to reduce their risk.

Answers: Chapter 3: Exercise 1

1. With so many express terms, the contract was 42 pages long.
2. The contractors and the suppliers were joint and severally liable under the contract.
3. Breaking a warranty doesn't necessarily mean the contract is void.
4. The campaign guidelines and schedule were set in accordance with the express terms of the contract.
5. The lawyer worded the conditions of the contract very carefully.
6. Most commercial contracts have a great number of "miscellaneous" clauses towards the back, which are often referred to as boilerplate clauses. Boilerplate clauses are often neglected during contract drafting and negotiation or in some cases only briefly reviewed, but this a mistake.
7. We read each and every clause of the sale of goods contract very carefully.
8. Liability was found to rest with the supplier because they failed to deliver the goods on time due to a series of errors in the supply chain.
9. The company enjoyed limited liability, so its directors' assets were protected.
10. They asked their lawyer to insert several exclusion clauses to reduce their risk.

3.2 Specific Terms: Section 2

There are two ways of drawing up contracts:

1. **Under seal (a deed)** (the parties sign the contract. This is witnessed, and it's made clear that it is executed as a deed)

2. **Under hand** (a 'simple contract' only signed by the parties in the contract).

To rely on or rely upon is: to depend on something to support yourself legally either in court or in negotiations.

A force majeure clause in a contract: is a special clause or provision, which means the parties do not have to carry out their obligations if circumstances outside of their control, such as natural disasters, mean that keeping to contractual duties is not possible for financial, legal or physical reasons.

When goods arrive to the customer in poor physical condition or damaged they are **defective.**

Plaintiff is a person who brings a case against another in court.

Remote Damage is any damage caused, but that could not have reasonably be predicted by the defendant. It also includes situations when the damage is not the typical result you would expect based on the defendant's actions. Under normal circumstances, a defendant would not usually be held responsible for remote damages to a person or property.

Share capital is the proportion of the capital of a company that comes from the issue of shares.

Bank balance is the amount of money held in a bank account at any specific moment in time.

We use the verb **practice** to describe the job that lawyers do. A practicing lawyer is a lawyer currently working as a lawyer. *Formerly, Mr. Jackson practiced in the bank's law department before moving to Manchester and practicing as a sole practitioner.*

The term of a contract explicitly states a fixed duration that the agreement will be in effect.

Free on board is a term which describes a transportation agreement whereby the vendor includes or assumes delivery without charge to a ship (or railway wagon). The buyer then assumes responsibility for transportation from that point.

In the United Kingdom, **corporation tax** is charged on the profits of limited companies.

Unit 3 Exercise 2: Vocabulary

Put the legal terms from the list below in the right gap. You might need to change the form of some words.

defective, corporation tax, practices, force majeure clause, plaintiff, bank balance, share capital, rely upon, legal fees, share capital, remote, free on board, contract under seal, deed, under hand, under seal, term, damage

Tax charged on companies' profits in the UK is called ....

Mr. John Cherry .... as a lawyer in TMF's London office.

The money a depositor has at a bank is that person's ....

.... is the capital invested in a company by its shareholders. ....
is a long-term source of finance for the company and in exchange for their investment, shareholders acquire a share of the ownership of the company.

The .... commenced an action for damages against Mayar Nabuko PLC.

The company refused to accept delivery of the books, because on inspection they were found to be ....

Rola Cola were unable to carry out the delivery before the due date as a result of flooding in one of their storage units. They have therefore .... the ....

Compensation for legal services provided by a lawyer or law firm for a client, in or out of court are called ....

A .... can also be referred to as a ....

Contracts can be executed .... or ....

The judge held that the .... Mr. Briggs had suffered was .... and therefore Mr. Ashford was found not liable under the law of contract.

The ....of the service contract with GDB Ltd is defined as 18 months.

If in the terms of sale, the price charged or quoted by a seller includes all delivery charges up to placing the goods on a ship at a port of departure specified by the buyer, we describe this as ....

Unit 3 Exercise 2: Vocabulary Answers

Tax charged on companies' profits in the UK is called corporation tax.

Mr. John Cherry practices as a lawyer in TMF's London office.

The money a depositor has at a bank is that person's bank balance.

Share capital is the capital invested in a company by its shareholders. Share capital is a long-term source of finance for the company and in exchange for their investment, shareholders acquire a share of the ownership of the company.

The plaintiff commenced an action for damages against Mayar Nabuko PLC.

The company refused to accept delivery of the books, because on inspection they were found to be defective.

Rola Cola were unable to carry out the delivery before the due date as a result of flooding in one of their storage units. They have therefore relied upon the force majeure clause.

Compensation for legal services provided by a lawyer or law firm for a client, in or out of court are called legal fees.

A deed can also be referred to as a contract under seal.

Contracts can be executed under seal or under hand.

The judge held that the damage Mr. Briggs had suffered was remote and therefore Mr. Ashford was found not liable under the law of contract.

The term of the service contract with GDB Ltd is defined as 18 months.

If in the terms of sale, the price charged or quoted by a seller includes all delivery charges up to placing the goods on a ship at a port of departure specified by the buyer, we describe this as free on board.

3.3 Specific Terms: Section 3: Setting up a Business

- You can set up a business and also set up as a sole trader, set up as a freelancer etc.. 'To set up' means 'to start'.

- The biggest drawback of setting up as a sole trader is that the person is legally liable for any debts they incur.

- If a sole trader doesn't pay his or her debts, they may lose assets such as their home, their car or their business premises.

- When you take out a loan you usually pay it back in instalments. For example, if you take out a loan for 5000 Euros at 0% interest and you pay it back in 10 monthly instalments, this means you have to pay 500 euros per month for a period of 10 months.

- An overdraft facility in a current account or business account is a pre-agreed deficit in a bank account which is caused by drawing more money than the account holds. It can be a useful tool for anyone, including for sole traders and small businesses.

- An outstanding loan is a loan that has not been paid yet. Similarly, an outstanding debt is a debt that hasn´t been paid.

- Interest rates are the percentage of interest on a loan that is charged to the borrower. Interest rates are normally expressed as an annual percentage of the loan outstanding.

- The terms and conditions of a contract are rules which a person or company must agree to respect in order to use a service.

- To indemnify is to pay compensation for damages caused.

- To hold harmless is to absolve a person or organization of responsibility for any damage or other liability arising from the transaction.

- A document describing the terms and conditions of an insurance agreement is called an insurance policy.

Unit 3 Exercise 3: Vocabulary

Put the legal terms from the list below in the right gap. You might need to change the form of some words.

insurance policy, hold harmless, take out, set up, indemnify, terms and conditions, interest rates, outstanding, asset, overdraft, liable, instalments

The document that provides details of the contract between an insurer and the person or organization that is insured is referred to as the ....

A .... clause is a provision in a contract, which states that an individual or organization is not liable for any injuries or damages that arise from signing the contract.

Since Mr. Powell was driving drunk, the insurance company would not .... him for the damage to his car.

Under the .... of the agreement, the buyer must ensure delivery of the goods before the first day of each month.

Higher .... may discourage people from spending money on cars.

Our account with the supplier has an .... debt of 420 euros. We need to pay it by June.

An .... facility in a bank account can be a useful tool for anyone, including for sole traders and small businesses.

The monthly .... on the loan I took out last year are quite reasonable. I only pay £50 a month.

I .... a loan for 75,000 Euros last year.

.... means legally responsible for something.

.... as a sole trader can be the fastest and easiest way to start a new business in many countries.

Examples of personal .... include a person´s home and other belongings.

Unit 3 Exercise 3: Vocabulary Answers

The document that provides details of the contract between an insurer and the person or organization that is insured is referred to as the insurance policy.

A hold harmless clause within a contract states that an individual or organization is not liable for any injuries or damages that arise from signing the contract.

Since Mr. Powell was driving drunk, the insurance company would not indemnify him for the damage to his car.

Under the terms and conditions of the agreement, the buyer must ensure delivery of the goods before the first day of each month.

Higher interest rates may discourage people from spending money on cars.

Our account with the supplier has an outstanding debt of 420 euros. We need to pay it by June.

An overdraft facility in a bank account can be a useful tool for anyone, including for sole traders and small businesses.

The monthly instalments on the loan I took out last year are quite reasonable. I only pay £50 a month.

I took out a loan for 75,000 Euros last year.

Liable means legally responsible for something.

Setting up as a sole trader can be the fastest and easiest way to start a new business in many countries.

Examples of personal assets include a person´s home and other belongings.

Chapter 4: Prepositions in Legal English

"Under" in Legal English & Contract Law

You should use *under* instead of *according to* or *pursuant to*, to refer to domestic or international substantive or procedural law. This also includes statutory and administrative law.

Examples:

Under current regulations the Commission only has to communicate to the local Council its "estimates" of expenditure for the forthcoming year.

Under U.S. contract law, parties to a contract possess the power to agree about the relief for breach of contract.

The definitions of the person skilled in the art given in Spanish Patent Law and in European Patent Convention are equivalent.

You can also use *under* when you refer to case law, or to any interpretations, doctrines and rules derived from case law:

The Commission plans to further clarify the conditions under which compensation can constitute state aid following the recent case law of the Court of Justice.

Source: Communication from the Commission to the European Parliament, the Council, the European Economic and Social Committee and the Committee of the Regions - White Paper on services of general interest: https://eur-lex.europa.eu/LexUriServ/LexUriServ.do?uri=CELEX:52004DC0374:EN:HTML

The notification was registered under the case number N 966/2013.

According to

Use *according to* when referring to testimonies and reported information.

According to the Guardian Newspaper, the US government has set out to extradite Mr. Howard Jones.

According to testimony presented by the independent expert, the financial reports had not been reviewed, otherwise the mistake would have been identified.

According to the report submitted by the local council, these projects had been submitted and approved long before the elaboration of the proposal.

Prepositions in Contract Law: Exercise 1

Read the following sentences and put a preposition in each space. Do NOT give more than one answer for each question.

You will hear from us (1) …….. 5 working days of us receiving your application.

The Buyer agrees to pay the fees in full and (2) …….. any deduction or withholding whatsoever on or before 1 September 2018.

The contract is being signed (3) …….. the Albert Street office at 1pm.

A material breach of the agreement was found to have occurred and the judge held that the claimant had grounds (4) …….. terminating the contract.

An event that occurs after a contract is signed which the parties could not have reasonably predicted and which is (5) ....their control is called supervening event.

The claim was brought (6) .... the company on the grounds of price fixing.

Being on someone's land without permission can be considered Tort of trespass (7) .... land.

Mr. Jones was party (8) .... confidential information belonging to his client and agreed to sign a non-disclosure agreement.

Following his prison sentence he was disqualified (9) .... driving a vehicle for 5 years.

The disputed invoice is (10) .... the amount of £6,000.

In 2015 inflation rates fell below 8% for the first time (11) …….. 7 years.

Answers:

You will hear from us (1) within 5 working days of us receiving your application.

The buyer agrees to pay the fees in full and (2) without any deduction or withholding on or before 1 September 2018.

The contract is being signed (3) at the Albert Street office at 1pm.

A material breach of the agreement was found to have occurred and the judge held that the claimant had grounds (4) for terminating the contract.

An event that occurs after a contract is signed which the parties could not have reasonably predicted and which is (5) beyond their control is called supervening event.

The claim was brought (6) against the company on the grounds of price fixing.

Being on someone's land without permission can be considered Tort of trespass (7) to land.

Mr. Jones was party (8) to confidential information belonging to his client and agreed to sign a non-disclosure agreement.

Following his prison sentence he was disqualified (9) from driving a vehicle for 5 years.

The disputed invoice is (10) in the amount of £6,000.

In 2015 inflation rates fell below 8% for the first time (11) in 7 years.

Prepositions in Contract Law: Exercise 2

Read the following sentences and put a preposition in each space. Do NOT give more than one answer for each question.

The parties ...... the agreement are Ben Sherwood and DMY Ltd.

We have been instructed ...... Mr. James Milner in connection with this matter.

Let me explain the background ...... the proposed transaction.

We are currently ...... discussions with two other firms with a view to setting up a joint venture.

Waterhouse has been instructed to advise Newcastle Sports Trust .... its primary care development project.

What effect will this new competitor have
…... your business?

Please provide us …... a list of transactions
carried out in last 3 months.

That is not really relevant …... the matter
under discussion.

May I draw your attention …... clause five of
the agreement?

The will must be signed …... the presence of
two people who are not to receive anything
under the terms of said will.

…... the event of non-repayment of the loan,
the bank will seek to enforce its security on
the property.

Answers:

The parties to the agreement are Ben Sherwood and DMY Ltd.

We have been instructed by Mr. James Milner in connection with this matter.

Let me explain the background of the proposed transaction.

We are currently in discussions with two other firms with a view to setting up a joint venture.

Waterhouse has been instructed to advise Newcastle Sports Trust about its primary care development project.

What effect will this new competitor have on your business?

Please provide us with a list of transactions carried out in last 3 months.

That is not really relevant to the matter under discussion.

May I draw your attention to clause five of the agreement?

The will must be signed in the presence of two people who are not to receive anything under the terms of said will.

In the event of non-repayment of the loan, the bank will seek to enforce its security on the property.

Prepositions in Contract Law: Exercise 3

Read the following sentences and put a preposition in each space. Do NOT give more than one answer for each question

Your full-time employment contract provides that you are entitled ….. 20 days holiday per year.

According to our records you are indebted to the company ….. the sum of 5,432 Euros.

We have sent a letter to Mr. Farlow in accordance …….. our client's instructions.

As a result of his accident, Mr. Patel decided to claim ……….. the company.

John Maclaen failed to make the repayments ….. the terms of his mortgage and the bank have initiated proceedings to repossess of their house.

We enclose a cheque for £6,000 in payment ….. your invoice dated 22 December 2016.

Any profits realized ……… excess of 15,000 will be subject to tax.

We are writing to inform you that, despite 2 reminders, we have not received payment ….. date and if this situation continues, we will have no alternative but to commence legal proceedings.

Instead of entering ………. a contract directly with their customers, some companies trade through an agency or distributorship agreement.

Answers:

Your full-time employment contract provides that you are entitled to 20 days holiday per year.

According to our records you are indebted to the company for the sum of 5,432 Euros.

We have sent a letter to Mr. Farlow in accordance with our client's instructions.

As a result of his accident, Mr. Patel decided to claim against the company.

John Maclean failed to make the repayments under the terms of his mortgage and the bank have initiated proceedings to repossess of their house.

We enclose a cheque for £6,000 in payment for your invoice dated 22 December 2016.

Any profits realized in excess of 15,000 will be subject to tax.

We are writing to inform you that, despite 2 reminders, we have not received payment to date and if this situation continues, we will have no alternative but to commence legal proceedings.

Instead of entering into a contract directly with their customers, some companies trade through agency or distributorship agreements.

Chapter 5: Legal English Phrasal Verbs Mini-dictionary with Practice Exercises

Read the definitions for each phrasal verb in section A below and complete the exercise at the end of the section.

A

Abide by means to accept or respect terms of an agreement, a law, a rule or a decision that has been made.

Accede to means to initially reject and then agree to a request after negotiation

Account for means:

(1) to provide an explanation of how or why something happened.

(2) To be a specific or named portion of something.

(3) To keep a record of and monitor how resources are used in a business.

(4) To take into consideration when you are making a decision.

Account to: to pay to an individual or organization together with a breakdown of the amount paid and how it is calculated.

Adhere to means to respect a particular law, rule, agreement or guidelines. (same as abide by)

Amount to means:

(1) to total or add up to.

(2) To be the same as.

Appertain to (or „pertain to") means to be related to or belong to something

Now complete each sentence with the most appropriate word or words. You may need to change the form of the words to suit the sentence and you will need to use some words more than once.

"The figures...................... to last year's sales.".

"When X Ltd failed to deliver the goods as specified under the agreement, this .... to a breach of contract"

"Both parties have .... strictly to the terms of the contract".

"The defendant .... to the claimant for damages received."

"There are 265 Euros which have not been .... for, we need to review the numbers again".

"Food sales .... 22% of total revenue".

"The potential tax bill if the case was lost was .... when we made the decision".

"All parties must .... the terms of the agreement"

"Last year, the supplier eventually
.....................repeated requests for an
increase in the line of credit".

"How can we ....the fact that
the goods arrived late?"

"The debt .... to over
€120,000".

B

Break down means:

(1) to separate information into several parts
to make it easier to understand, analyze and
discuss.

(2) To fail.

Break off means: (1) to stop negotiating or
discussing

Break up means: (1) the separation of a company or an organization into smaller parts.

Complete each sentence with the most appropriate word or words. You may need to change the form of the words to suit the sentence and you will need to use some words more than once.

"The agreement .... due to one party´s excessive demands".

"We had to .... the meeting".

"The company was .... to make the sector more competitive"

"The numbers for the year .... as follows"

E

Enter into means (1) to begin or start a formal agreement; or (2) to start to deal with something.

Entitle to (Adj. Entitled to) means to give the right to something.

Exclude (noun form: an exclusion): When something is not covered, as in specific damage not covered in a contract.

Complete each sentence with the most appropriate word or words. You may need to change the form of the words to suit the sentence and you will need to use some words more than once.

"Both parties shall have the right to seek to settle any dispute arising from the agreement by arbitration, which will .... any other form of dispute resolution."

"Ms. Temple .... negotiations with the factory to reach an agreement."

"Early termination of the contract
………………..the lender to compensation".

F

Factor in: to include or take into account
when assessing, evaluating or planning
something.

Find in favor of/Against (also: Rule in favor
of/against) is often used to describe the
decision of the judge or jury in court.

**Complete each sentence with the most
appropriate word or words. You may need
to change the form of the words to suit
the sentence and you will need to use
some words more than once.**

"The judge ……………………… Mr. Right
and awarded him compensation to the
amount of £10,000"

"Using a computer program they
…………………………. the costs of keeping
the old machinery for the next three years"

H

Hand Down:

(1) In inheritance, this phrasal verb means to give or leave something to someone else.

(2) When a judge or jury announce their official decision in a case.

Complete each sentence with the most appropriate word or words. You may need to change the form of the words to suit the sentence and you will need to use some words more than once.

"The judge .... a suspended sentence"

"The land .... to him by his uncle, who died last year".

P

Pass off means:

'Passing off' is also a type of tort, which for example restricts businesses from giving the impression that their goods or services are associated with another.

Provide that...

If you are giving a detailed summary, paraphrasing, or repeating a particular law word for word, use "provide (s) that"

Complete each sentence with the most appropriate word or words. You may need to change the form of the words to suit the sentence and you will need to use some words more than once.

"The law .... that the penalty for a first offence can be up to 150 USD."

"She was accused of trying to .... her logo for another company's".

"The Regulations ....
"traffic data" must be recorded and filed with the appropriate agency. "

S

Set forth is used before words such as rights, duties, obligations, and procedures:

Strike Out means (1) this is when a judge suspends a case before the court date.

Sum Up to sum up means to summarize information. In legal English 'the summing up' in a trial with a jury, is when the judge summarizes the evidence presented, in order to draw the attention of the jury to the most important points.

Complete each sentence with the most appropriate word or words. You may need to change the form of the words to suit the sentence and you will need to use some words more than once.

"The judge .... the evidence presented by both sides before the jury made their decision"

"The Regulation .... the procedure for processing and fulfilment of orders"

"Articles 12 and 22 can unite the parties and contribute to advancing regional priorities within the framework .... by the law."

"The judge can .... the case if she decides there finds no reasonable grounds"

"The following article .... the basic terms of the contract."

W

Weigh up is to evaluate evidence and arguments before making a decision.

Complete the sentence with the most appropriate word or words. You may need to change the form of the words to suit the sentence and you will need to use some words more than once.

"The judge …………………….. the evidence for over an hour before handing down her verdict."

Exercise Answers:

A

"The figures appertain to last year's sales.".

"When X Ltd failed to deliver the goods as specified under the agreement, this amounted to a breach of contract"

"Both parties have adhered strictly to the terms of the contract".

"The defendant accounted to the claimant for damages received."

"There are 265 Euros which have not been accounted for, we need to review the numbers again".

"Food sales accounted for 22% of total revenue".

"The potential tax bill if the case was lost was accounted for when we made the decision".

"All parties must abide by the terms of the agreement"

"Last year, the supplier eventually acceded to repeated requests for an increase in the line of credit".

"How can we account for the fact that the goods arrived late?"

"The debt amounted to over €120,000".

B

"The agreement broke down due to one party´s excessive demands".

"We had to break off the meeting".

"The company was broken up to make the sector more competitive"

"The numbers for the year break down as follows"

E

"Both parties shall have the right to seek to settle any dispute arising from the agreement by arbitration, which will exclude any other form of dispute resolution."

"Ms. Temple entered into negotiations with the factory to reach an agreement."

"Early termination of the contract entitles the lender to compensation".

F

"The judge found in favor of Mr. Right and awarded him compensation to the amount of £10,000"

"Using a computer program they factored in the costs of keeping the old machinery for the next three years"

H

"The judge handed down a suspended sentence"

"The land was handed down to him by his uncle, who died last year".

P

"The law provides that the penalty for a first offence can be up to 150 USD."

"She was accused of trying to pass off her logo for another company's".

"The Regulations provide that "traffic data" must be recorded and filed with the appropriate agency. "

S

"The judge summed up the evidence presented by both sides before the jury made their decision"

"The Regulation sets forth the procedure for processing and fulfilment of orders"

"Articles 12 and 22 can unite the parties and contribute to advancing regional priorities within the framework set forth by the law."

"The judge can strike out the case if she decides that there are no reasonable grounds"

"The following article sets forth the basic terms of the contract."

W

"The judge weighed up the evidence for over an hour before handing down her verdict."

Chapter 6.

Communicating Clearly:

Active VS Passive

Active Voice

It's a good idea to use the active voice if possible, as it makes for more organized, clear, and vivid sentences in general. Passive voice sentences are often longer and use more obscure word combinations, but they're also less specific and can lead to disconnected readers.

Examples:

Simple Present

Active: *Mary Higgins handles the new accounts.*

Passive: *The new accounts are handled (by Mary Higgins).*

Present Continuous

Active: *Mary Higgins is handling the new accounts.*

Passive: *The new accounts are being handled (by Mary Higgins).*

Simple Past

Active: *Mary Higgins handled the new accounts.*

Passive: *The new accounts were handled (by Mary Higgins).*

Present Perfect

Active: *Mary Higgins has handled the new accounts.*

Passive: *The new accounts have been handled (by Mary Higgins).*

Past Perfect

Active: *Mary Higgins had handled the new accounts.*

Passive: *The new accounts had been handled (by Mary Higgins).*

Future

Active: *Mary Higgins will handle the new accounts.*

Passive: *The new accounts will be handled (by Mary Higgins).*

Auxiliary Verb "Must"

Active: *Mary Higgins must handle the new accounts.*

Passive: *The new accounts must be handled (by Mary Higgins).*

Passive Voice

The active voice usually is more straightforward and more potent than the passive:

Most of our New York office will be attending the conference.

This is clearer and more concise than:

The conference will be attended by most of our New York office.

Using the passive when it is not necessary can sometimes produce ridiculous sentences like:

The conference will be attended by me next week.

If you try to tidy up this passive sentence by removing "*by me,*" you turn it into an indefinite:

The conference will be attended next week.

The sentence is now too unclear.

Who is going to be attending the conference?

Is it an unknown group of people?

Are we referring to people in general?

It's always better to write and say: *I will be attending the conference next week.*

Summary:

- Use the active voice most of the time.

- The active voice carries more power, particularly in writing.

Many weak statements can be made lively and emphatic by using a verb in the active voice and avoiding fillers like *'the reason why' or 'the reason that...'*.

Examples:

The reason why she resigned from her last role was that her health became impaired.

It would be much better to express the above sentence as:

Failing health compelled her to resign from her last role.

It wasn't too long before I felt regret for how I'd behaved.

It would be much better to express the above sentence as:

I soon regretted my behavior.

How to Avoid Conflict & Be Diplomatic

The passive voice gets a terrible reputation, partly because so many people overuse it to portray a 'professional tone,' and end up using it incorrectly. This doesn't mean that you should completely discard it, as it is often convenient and necessary in business and legal writing.

Contrary to what many writing books would have you believe, the passive voice is vital when you need to draw focus away from the person performing the action. Maybe the person or thing that performs the action isn't significant, or it could even be a sensitive or delicate matter. Using the passive voice is especially useful for texts where you need to come across as objective, such as legal texts or company policies and regulations.

As Mr. Friedrich Nietzsche once said, *"we often refuse to accept an idea merely because the tone in which it has been expressed is unsympathetic to us."*

Take the following example:

You must not leave the door open at any time.

This sentence is clear and direct, but it also sounds confrontational and condescending.

The door must not be left open at any time is a better option.

Similarly:

We will not include accessories

is saying: *'we, the greedy, difficult company who want to sell you this product to make money off you, are denying you all the accessories that we have just shown you in this product picture so that you have to go and buy them separately and we can make more money off you.'*

It's more impersonal and less confrontational if we simply use the passive voice and write.

Accessories (are) not included.

There are other situations where you may wish to focus the reader's thinking on a subject that is receiving an action. In the following active voice sentence:

We will donate 75,000 USD

the most important focus of the sentence (the 75,000 USD) doesn't appear until the end. Meanwhile,

Over 75,000 USD will be donated

is written in the passive voice, but it starts with the most important information and really changes the focus in the reader's mind. It's literally more bang for your buck. So, passive or active? It all depends on the message you have and your business objective.

Try not to make one passive verb depend directly on another in a sentence.

They have been proven to have been investigated by authorities.

The sentence above would be better if we changed it to:

It has been proven that they were investigated by authorities.

Or

It has been proven that authorities investigated them.

A typical inefficiency in passive sentences is to write a noun that expresses the entire action of the sentence as the subject. If we do this, we have no choice but to use a redundant verb that adds no meaning to the sentence.

An analysis of the infrastructure was done in 2019.

VS

The infrastructure was analyzed in 2019.

Summary:

Use the Passive

1. To emphasize the action itself instead of the Person or Thing that 'Does' the Action.

"After four days of negotiations, an agreement was reached by the managing partners."

2. To Be Tactful

"The events were misconstrued."

"Mistakes were made."

3. When the doer is unknown or not important

"Every month, hundreds of people are left homeless."

4. To Set a Detached or Official Tone (Signs or Notices)

"Guests are not allowed to smoke."

Converting from Passive to Active Voice

1. Move the doer of the action to the start of the sentence and move the person or thing that receives the action after the verb.

2. Adapt the verb form as needed.

3. If no doer is mentioned in the passive sentence, you can often logically infer who or what acted.

   For example, in the sentence.

   All of Nike's factories were pulled out of China.

   Even though we haven't explicitly said that *Nike* pulled the factories out of China, it is implied in the sentence that since we haven't mentioned the person or group who pulled them out, it must be Nike itself. Therefore, *Nike* is the doer, and the factories are the object that receives the action.

All of Nike's factories were pulled out of China.

Nike pulled all its factories out of China.

You have to do the exact opposite if you want to change an active sentence into a passive one.

For example:

Do not close the window.

The window should not be closed.

Or in the positive

The window should be kept open at all times.

Exercise

Decide whether each of the following sentences is active or passive. If you think the sentence doesn't need changing, just write "no change" next to it. If you think changing it from active to passive or vice-versa would improve it, go ahead and rewrite the sentence.

1. Staff don't speak English at the front desk.

....

....

2. A report was given to him by Mary.

....

....

3. Many people know Bavaria for its cuisine.

....

....

4. You should reconsider the new policy you are trying to implement.

....

....

Answers

1. **Staff don't speak English at the front desk.**

   No change is needed here, usually. This can be expressed as a complaint or a simple observation, depending on the tone of voice.

2. **A report was given to him by Mary.**

   Mary gave him a report.

3. **Many people know Bavaria for its cuisine.**

   Bavaria is known for its cuisine.

4. **You need to change the new policy you are trying to implement.**

   The new policy needs to be changed.

   This is much less personal and confrontational.

Chapter 7. Language &

Punctuation Rules

Possessives & Apostrophes

Make the possessive singular of nouns by adding *'s,* whatever the final consonant.

For example:

Charles's colleague

Burns's email

the project's main goal

Exceptions:

You may also encounter nouns that finish with an 's' written like this: 'Charles' colleague' and 'Burns' email. Writing it like this, is also generally acceptable, but if you're not sure, it's best to follow the initial example and simply add 's regardless of what the final consonant is.

Other possible exceptions are the possessives of ancient proper names ending in -es and -is, the possessive *Jesus',* and some forms like *for conscience' sake, for righteousness' sake.*

Possessives such as *hers, his, yours,* ours, theirs, its and

oneself do not carry apostrophe.

Lists

In a list of three or more things with a single conjunction, use a comma after each term. You can choose to use an Oxford comma* before the last one or not, depending on your preference, but be aware that it could make some sentences unclear.

Example:

laptops, phones, and other electronic devices

wine, beer, or spirits

They opened the meeting, discussed the main issues concerning the project, and left before we were able to raise our concerns.

*The Oxford Comma

The Oxford comma is a comma placed before the last item in a series of three or more. Many style guides advise against using it, and many style guides advise writers to use it. For practical reasons, this guide advises in favor of using it, as it can avoid miscommunication in some instances. For example, *I have received confirmation from the engineering team, Thom and Joe.*

This is ambiguous, as we might not know whether the engineering team are Tom and Joe, or whether Thom and Joe are separate entities in the list. It's much clearer; therefore, to write, *I have received confirmation from the engineering team, Tom, and Joe.*

If you're interested in seeing the potential business issues that misusing the Oxford comma can cause, search online for the case of the Oxford comma dispute settled for $5 million!

Business Names

In the names of businesses, the last comma is usually omitted,

Brown, Shipley & Co.

Adding Information with Parenthetical Expressions

Enclose parenthetical expressions between commas.

The best way to see Berlin, unless you are pressed for time, is to walk around the center.

- If there is very little interruption to the sentence flow, you don't need to add commas.

- What you can't do is add one comma and omit the other.

Examples of wrong use of commas in this case are:

The project founder, Jack Glibb sent me an email yesterday,

or

Jack Glibb you will be pleased to hear, is coming to New York for the meeting,...

If there is a conjunction before a parenthetic expression, put the first comma before the conjunction, not after it.

He welcomed me into his office, and unaware that I had already spoken about the matter with his manager, (he) proceeded to tell me all about the new project.

Days and Dates

The following are always parenthetic and should be enclosed between commas (or, at the end of the sentence, between comma and period):

- Years that form part of a date.

- Days of the month that appear after the day of the week.

June 12, 1999

September to November, 2019.

Wednesday, September 16, 2020.

Abbreviations like *Jr.* and *etc.* follow the same rule.

Non-restrictive Relative Clauses

Relative clauses that don't help us identify the noun that went before them, and other clauses indicating time or location of events.

Example:

The manager, who had initially been quite hostile, became a lot friendlier once we explained our idea.

In this sentence, the clause '*who had initially been quite hostile*' doesn't specify one manager from a group of two or more managers; there's only one manager present in the situation described.

The sentence combines two separate statements to provide complete information. The clause '*who had initially been quite hostile*' gives extra information for a fuller picture of the situation's dynamics. It could even be expressed as two separate sentences, but it wouldn't be as efficient:

The manager had initially been quite hostile. He became friendlier once we'd explained our idea.

With different punctuation, the meaning is different. Compare the various meanings of these two sentences:

The manager, who had initially been quite hostile, became a lot friendlier once we explained our idea.

VS.

The manager who had at first been quite hostile, became friendlier once we explained our idea.

In the second sentence, we're talking about a particular manager from a group of possible managers present during the meeting. We can't divide this sentence into two statements like we could with the first example.

Dependent Clauses

Phrases or dependent clauses that go just before or after the main clause of a sentence.

Partly through smart investments, partly through joint ventures, they have managed to grow their profits by 40% in the last twelve months and have become pioneers with the release of their new software, as well as the opening of a new call-center.

Comma before conjunctions that introduce co-ordinate clauses.

The economic outlook is bleak, but there is still one chance of avoiding disaster.

The above sentence is perfectly acceptable, but it can give the impression of being a little unprofessional sometimes, mainly when we use this style repeatedly. It gives the impression of being improvised and slightly lazy if we just use the same structure over and over.

The sentence could be rewritten as follows:

Although the economic outlook is bleak, there is still one chance of avoiding disaster.

Or we could switch the subordinate clauses for phrases:

In this bleak economic outlook, there is still one chance of avoiding disaster.

Offering Relief

You need to offer your reader some relief at times.

If you make your sentences too uniformly compact and periodic, the style becomes too robotic, formal, and solemn without an occasional loose sentence. It is best to use a combination of all three structures given above.

Dependent clauses, or introductory phrases set off by a comma, which go

before the second independent clause, do not need a comma after the conjunction.

Example: *The economic outlook is bleak, but if we are prepared to act promptly, there is still one chance of avoiding disaster.*

Independent Clauses

Independent clauses in a sentence

If you need to write a single sentence with two or more grammatically complete clauses that are not joined by a conjunction, use a semicolon instead of a comma.

James's presentations are entertaining; they are full of valuable information.

It's nearly half-past five; we cannot reach the meeting room before half-past six.

You can also write each of the above examples as two separate sentences:

James's presentations are entertaining. They are full of valuable information.

It's nearly half-past five. We cannot reach the meeting room before half-past six.

Use a comma if you add a conjunction.

James's presentations are entertaining, as they are full of valuable information.

It's nearly half-past five, and we cannot reach the meeting room before half-past six.

Participial Phrases

If you use a participial phrase at the start of a sentence, it must refer to the person or thing that performs the action in that sentence.

Talking to Jenna, I realized that I need a new challenge.

The word *talking* refers to the doer of the sentence (*me* in this case), not to Jenna.

The same rules apply when you start sentences with participial phrases that carry a conjunction, preposition, noun in apposition, adjective, or adjective phrase before them.

On arriving in Chicago, my assistant met me at the station.

VS

When I arrived (or, On my arrival) in Chicago, my assistant met me at the station.

A manager with a proven track record, they have entrusted him with setting up the new department.

VS

A manager with a proven track record, he has been entrusted with setting up the new department.

Avoid Loose Sentences

Although a loose sentence now and then can be useful to provide relief for the reader, a series of them soon becomes monotonous and tedious. Therefore, if you aim for a semi-formal or formal tone, try to avoid using too many loose sentences.

People often write whole paragraphs around loose sentences, using: *but, and, so, which,* who, *where, when,* and *while.*

The third presentation of the conference was given this afternoon, and a large audience was in attendance. Mr. Edward Appleton spoke first about his team's findings, and his colleague Ms. Freda Burns presented the supporting evidence. The former showed himself to be very knowledgeable in his field, while the latter proved herself fully deserving of her excellent reputation. The interest aroused by the presentation has been very gratifying to the Committee, and it is planned to hold a similar conference annually hereafter. The fourth presentation will be given on Tuesday, May 4, when an equally fascinating program will be presented.

The paragraph above can be improved by injecting some variety into the sentence structures.

Suppose you find that you have written a series of sentences of the type described. In that case, you can edit enough of them to remove the monotony, replacing them with simple sentences, with sentences of two clauses joined by a semicolon, with periodic sentences of two clauses, periodic or loose sentences, of three clauses-whichever best expresses your ideas.

Similar Meaning and Function
Should Have a Similar Form

It's best to have a similar form and structure for sentences that carry a similar meaning or function within the paragraph. This helps the reader identify and understand the information more smoothly and provides a better overall reading experience.

If you need to repeat a sentence to emphasize it, you might need to vary its form, but otherwise, try to keep your structures the same for sentences with a similar function. For example: if you're giving solutions, then all of them should have a similar grammatical form so that the reader can automatically identify them.

Exercise

Revise the following sentences to reflect consistent grammatical construction for the similar ideas expressed.

1. There is a considerable gap in the market for fashionable mountain wear among the Swiss, the Italians, the Spanish, and French.

....

....

....

....

2. Either you must query the invoice or provide payment.

....

....

....

....

3. Our client has ample experience in the South East Asian markets and in Japan.

....

....

....

....

4. It was both a long meeting and very tedious.

....

....

....

....

Answers

1. There is a considerable gap in the market for fashionable mountain wear among the Swiss, the Italians, the Spanish, and French.

    There is a considerable gap in the market for fashionable mountain wear among the Swiss, Italians, Spanish, and French.

2. Either you must query the invoice or provide payment.

    You must either query the invoice or provide payment.

3. Our client has ample experience in the South East Asian markets and in Japan.

    Our client has ample experience in the South East Asian and Japanese markets.

4. It was both a long meeting and very tedious.

    The meeting was both long and tedious.

Parentheses

If you add parentheses in the middle of a sentence to give extra information, use the same punctuation you would if the parentheses were absent.

Examples

I went to his office yesterday (my third attempt to see him), but he had left early.

She suggests (but with what evidence?) that a less aggressive pitch would be more effective with this client.

(If you need to add a full stop to the phrase in parentheses, the stop is placed inside the closing parenthesis.)

Quotations

Providing Evidence in Formal Reports and Emails

If you need to add direct quotations in formal writing, introduce them with a colon and then add the quotation marks.

Example

The provision of the contract is: "The first 5-year period has hard call protection."

*Vocabulary Note: Hard Call Protection

Hard call protection, or absolute call protection, is a provision included in callable bonds, which states that the bond issuer must wait until an agreed date before redeeming the bond.

Quotes that Do Not Provide Formal Evidence Within a Sentence

Seth Godin coined the phrase, "There's no shortage of remarkable ideas, what's missing is the will to execute them."

As Phil Knight said, "Play by the rules but be ferocious."

Begin a quotation of a full sentence or paragraph on a new line and center it, but there's no need for quotation marks.

Example

We can learn a lot from the words of President Obama:

The real test is not whether you avoid this failure because you won't. It's whether you let it harden or shame you into inaction, or whether you learn from it; whether you choose to persevere.

Quotations introduced by *that* are regarded as indirect and not placed within quotation marks.

Example

I can see from Branson's report that all the relevant safety measures have been adhered to.

Cliché expressions and famous phrases from popular culture do not need quotation marks.

Two heads are better than one.

Chapter 8. Word Order

Where you choose to arrange words in a sentence communicates their relationship. If feasible, keep words and groups of words connected in meaning and separate the ones that don't share a close connection.

There's a large reservoir in the area that we need to build around.

Should read:

We need to build around a large reservoir in the area.

Exercise

Rewrite the following sentence by reorganizing the words to make it clearer. You can check the suggested answer on the next page.

Wallace, in his latest report that he sent to us last month, gave a full justification for the recent overspend.

Should read:

....

....

....

....

Answer

Wallace, in his latest report that he sent to us last month, gave a full justification for the recent overspend.

In his latest report last month, Wallace gave a full justification for the recent overspend.

Stick to the Word Order Rule

Although it often causes no issues in shorter, more straight forward sentences, you should stick to this rule because the interposed phrase or clause needlessly interrupts the natural order of the main clause. This can cause confusion and miscommunication when dealing with longer, more complex sentences. In the first example above, when we read the sentence *"there's a large reservoir in the area that we need to build around,"* we cannot possibly know for certain whether the writer is saying that we need to build around the area or whether he or she is saying that we need to build around the reservoir. The second version of this sentence leaves no room for interpretation: *"We need to build around a large reservoir in the area."*

As a rule, the relative pronoun should come immediately after its antecedent.

He wrote an article about his recent project, which was published in May's newsletter.

Should read:

He published an article in May's newsletter about his recent project.

This is the Chicago headquarters of Push Co., which is the subsidiary of S.P. Inc. It supplies the entire state of Illinois.

Should read:

This is the Chicago headquarters of Push Co., a subsidiary of S.P. Inc., which supplies the entire state of Illinois.

To avoid ambiguity, the following example should be rewritten.

A report to analyze the performance of our social media campaigns this year, which have produced varied results...

Instead, it should read:

A report to analyze the varied results of our social media campaigns this year...

Modifiers need to be, whenever feasible, with the word they are modifying.

All the members were not present.

Should read:

Not all the members were present.

He only found two mistakes.

Should read

He found only two mistakes.

Exercise

Rearrange the following sentence so that the modifiers are next to the word they are modifying.

Andrew Joyce will give a talk on Tuesday morning in Conference Room B, to which all staff members are invited, on the updated pay structure at 11 A.M.

....

....

....

....

Answer

Andrew Joyce will give a talk on Tuesday morning in Conference Room B, to which all staff members are invited, on the updated pay structure at 11 A.M.

On Tuesday morning at 11 A.M., Andrew Joyce will give in Conference room B a talk on the updated pay structure. All staff members are invited.

Some of these corrected examples may seem slightly unnatural to you, however they are a great way of avoiding any miscommunications.

For example, the sentence:

On Tuesday morning at 11 A.M., Andrew Joyce will give in Conference room B a talk on the updated pay structure. All staff members are invited.

Can be expressed as:

On Tuesday morning at 11 A.M. in Conference room B, Andrew Joyce will give a talk on the updated pay structure. All staff members are invited.

This would not cause any confusion and is a very logical way of expressing the information. However, if you apply this structure in the following sentence:

On Tuesday morning at 11 A.M. in Rome, Andrew Joyce will give a virtual talk on the updated pay structure. All staff members are invited.

The problem with the above structure is that we now don't know whether the writer is telling us that the talk is at 11 A.M. local time in Rome or 11 A.M. wherever we are. There is an ambiguity which can lead to problems.

Therefore, the sentence should read:

On Tuesday morning at 11 A.M., Andrew Joyce will give in Rome a virtual talk on the updated pay structure. All staff members are invited.

OR

On Tuesday morning at 11 A.M., Andrew Joyce will give a virtual talk from Rome on the updated pay structure. All staff members are invited.

Chapter 9. How to Summarize Information

Unless you are describing future forecasts, when summarizing, you should preferably use the present tense or the past tense, depending on which is more suitable. If you use the present tense, express past events in the present perfect; if you use the past, in past perfect.

As a result of the circumstances outlined above, this project cannot be delivered by the agreed deadline. My team and I have made every effort to avoid this delay and offer our sincerest apologies for any inconvenience caused.

A past tense in indirect communication must remain in its original tense.

The manufacturers accept that their machinery was at fault.

Apart from the exceptions noted, whichever tense you choose, use throughout. Changing from one tense to another looks disorganized and takes power away from your communication.

In presenting the statements or the thoughts of someone else, as in summarizing a report or a speech, avoid inserting expressions like "s*he stated*," "she *added*," "*the speaker then went on to say*," or any other similar phrase. Instead of wasting words by constantly telling the reader or listener that "s*he stated*," "she *added*," or "*the speaker then went on to say*," inform your audience that you are providing a summary and then focus on communicating the important information.

Chapter 10. Subject-Verb Agreement

The subject of any sentence we write must coincide with the verb form we use. If the doer of the action in our sentence is plural, then the verb must be written in its plural form. The same applies the other way, so if the doer of the action is singular, then the verb form must also be singular.

For example:

*"**The writ** of execution **was** canceled."*

*"**The accounts were** forged."*

Collective Nouns

In American English, collective nouns are treated as singular entities.

Example: "*The **team is** losing all **its** players to injury.*"

Collective nouns can be treated as singular or plural in British English, though most British writers will gravitate towards the plural form.

Example: "*The **team are** losing all **their** players to injury.*"

Another example might be:

"*The **gift deeds were** submitted six days ago.*"

VS.

"*The **file with the gift deeds was** submitted six days ago.*"

This seems straightforward, but there can be issues when the collective noun is less clear.

Exercise:

Why is there a grammatical difference between *'a file'* and *'a number of'* or *'several'*? They are both collective nouns that refer to more than one individual within that collective. So, why the difference? Read the following two sentences and think about your answer. When you are ready, check your answer under the Answer section.

Sentence 1: *"The <u>file with the gift deeds was</u> submitted six days ago."*

VS.

Sentence 2: *"Several gift deeds were submitted six days ago."*

Answer:

In Sentence 1, the focal point of the message is 'the file.' We submitted the file, and there is only one file, so it's singular. However, in Sentence 2, the focus is on 'the deeds.' This is `plural.

This answer might be frustrating to some readers, as there are many nuances that can change the grammar of a sentence in English.

To go one step further and illustrate this, let's look at the following example:

"The number of gift deeds we drafted last year was much higher."

Exercise:

Why is *'the number of'* in the answer above suddenly singular?

We are still referring to more than one deed, so why is it now being treated as singular? Look at both sentences and think about your answer. When you are ready, check the Answer section.

Sentence 2: "*A number of gift deeds were submitted six days ago.*"

Sentence 3: "The *number of gift deeds we drafted last year was much higher.*"

Answer:

The answer to this is the focus once more. Sentence 2, as we saw, focuses on the plurality of the deeds. Meanwhile, Sentence 3 focuses on the change to 'the number.' Was the number higher or lower? It was higher. If we focus on the change to this number, we need to treat it as singular because it's a singular number.

It's also worth noting that some nouns can be treated as singular or plural depending on preference.

Example:

Charity

Private Limited Company

Public Limited Company

Option 1: *Alpha Beta Charlie PLC __are__ __producers__ of free-range animal products.*

VS.

Option 2: *Alpha Beta Charlie PLC is a producer of free-range animal products.*

Both the above options are 100% correct. However, since a company is considered a separate individual legal entity, the norm is to express these nouns in the singular when discussing legal matters.

When referring to nouns like:

✔ Prosecution

✔ Jury

✔ Corporation

We can choose whether we write about them in singular or plural. The important thing is to remain consistent. We must choose a practice and stick to it as much as possible, especially within the same document.

Mixture of Singular and Plural Nouns

In the following example, several forms were sent to the NY office.

Therefore, we use the plural:

*"The non-disclosure agreement, the corporate bylaws, and the purchase agreement **were** all sent to our New York office on 23rd March."*

However, if we rewrite this sentence to focus the reader's attention on one particular document:

*"The non-disclosure agreement **was** sent to our New York office, **together with** corporate bylaws and the purchase agreement on 23rd March."*

The sentence's subject is now the *non-disclosure agreement,* so the verb needs to be singular.

When the subject of the sentence is an 'indefinite pronoun,' like the word *'each,'* we treat it as singular.

For example: *"**Each** of the forms **has** been filled out and sent to the relevant office."*

Sentences with Two Subjects

If the two subjects are singular, the verb stays singular:

*"Neither the <u>employment contract</u> nor the <u>loan agreement</u> **were** sent on time."*

Should be written as:

*"Neither the <u>employment contract</u> nor the <u>loan agreement</u> **was** sent on time."*

If one of the subjects is plural, we use a plural verb.

*"Neither the <u>employment contracts</u> nor the <u>loan agreement</u> **were** sent on time."*

*"Neither the <u>employment contract</u> nor the <u>loan agreements</u> **were** sent on time."*

Chapter 11. Verbs Versus Nouns

When we turn a base verb into a noun, this is called "nominalization." While it is very useful when we want to add variety to our professional writing, it can sometimes affect the power and meaning of our sentences.

Very noun-heavy sentences tend to be more watered-down in meaning since verbs carry more urgency and power.

They are also less direct and longer, sometimes making them convoluted.

Examples:

The court **made the decision to grant** *an injunction against Sean McFarlane after careful consideration.*

The court **granted** *an injunction against Sean McFarlane after careful consideration.*

The second sentence is better since it's clearer, more direct, and shorter.

Key Word Transformation Exercise:

The following sentences are quite noun-heavy and would be better expressed more directly. Transform them to make them clearer and more concise.

The considerable increase in crime over the past year has led to pressure being put on the police force (for a solution).

The removal of the ambiguities in the contract made it look much clearer.

Answers

Crime has increased considerably over the past year, and the police force is under pressure to find a solution.

The ambiguities in the contract were removed, which made it much clearer.

Chapter 12. Ending a Sentence with a Preposition

This traditional guideline also comes from a rule used in Latin, where it is grammatically incorrect and nonsensical to end any sentence with a preposition. In many Romance languages, putting a preposition at the end of a sentence can make it unintelligible in many cases.

In English, on the other hand, it depends on the audience. Some readers adhere to this guideline strictly and, in some cases, will judge your writing to be sloppy if you end a sentence with a preposition. Therefore, if we are writing for a more traditional audience, we might want to avoid ending our sentences with prepositions.

Examples:

Option 1: Ending with a preposition

Advantages: More relaxed, direct, and clearer sentences.

Disadvantage: Might be judged poorly by some more traditional readers.

Example: *She is one of the few secretaries he enjoys working with.*

Option 2: Restructuring your sentence to avoid ending with a preposition

Advantages: Much more formal. It will satisfy more traditional readers.

Disadvantage: It depends on the type of writing. It can be quite impersonal in some cases, like in semi-formal emails to colleagues or clients. It is not as direct and clear as ending with a preposition in most cases.

Example: *She is one of the few secretaries with whom he enjoys working.*

The Problem with Obsessing Over the Preposition Guideline

English isn't Latin and is not structured in the same way as Italian, Spanish, etc. Therefore, the rules that apply there aren't always fully transferable to English.

When we speak, we do not always know how we will end our sentences. There are idioms and phrasal verbs in English that require the speaker or the writer to end some sentences with prepositions. This is not imposed by artificial, arbitrary rules; it's a requirement of real-world communication. It's important to remember that this is exactly what a language is designed to do. English is and should always be a constantly evolving tool for effective, purposeful communication. If we abandon this primary goal, we start to lose sight of what is important. As Winston Churchill once said, *"Correcting my grammar is something up with which I will not put."*

Chapter 13. "That" & "Which"

We use *"that"* to add a clause that defines exactly what we are talking or writing about. This clause should narrow the focus of the topic we are treating.

We use *"which"* to connect a clause that doesn't add extra focus on the discussion topic. This clause doesn't narrow down the topic.

Although *"that"* and *"which"* are often treated interchangeably in spoken English, when we are writing, our readers do not have the luxury of being able to infer meaning from our tone of voice and pauses. Therefore, it is vitally important that we pay attention to this rule.

The following two sentences illustrate the significance of using *"that"* and *"which"* correctly in writing:

Example 1: *The evidence **that** Mr. Miyagui presented to the judge was far from reliable.*

Meaning: This sentence means that of the larger body of evidence, the specific evidence presented by Mr. Miyagui wasn't reliable.

Example 2: *The evidence, **which** Mr. Miyagui presented to the judge, was far from accurate.*

Meaning: This sentence means that Mr. Miyagui presented all the evidence available, and it wasn't reliable.

As you can see, there is a huge difference in meaning here.

Chapter 14. Conjunctions

As we saw earlier in this book, we can connect two ideas or concepts in a single sentence, as long as we use the right conjunction. Conjunctions are essentially words that connect.

Look at the following example, which is missing a conjunction:

"The notice was served on 21 July, no response has been received."

How can you fix this sentence? Rewrite it below:

Answer:

The sentence would be better if we wrote it as follows:

"The notice was served on 21 July, **but** *no response has been received."*

In the answer above, the two parts of the sentence are linked by the conjunction **'but.'**

We could also start the sentence with '*although*':

Rewrite the sentence using the word '*although.*'

Answer:

"***Although*** *the notice was delivered on 21 July, no response has been received.*"

We can also express the same meaning using punctuation.

In the above example, we could use a **semicolon:**

Rewrite the sentence using a semicolon:

Answer:

"The notice was served on 21 July; no response has been received."

We can also use two sentences instead of one by using *'However'*:

Split the original sentence into two sentences using the word *'However.'*

Answer:

"The notice was served on 21 July. **However,** *no response has been received."*

Please Note: there should be a full stop or a semicolon in front of *'however'* if it introduces a new clause.

Chapter 15. Ambiguous & Misused Modifiers

Words and groups of words that describe other words or groups of words are called 'modifiers.' We need to include any modifiers as closely as we can to the words they describe. Misplacing modifiers can lead to major misunderstandings and ambiguity.

Case Study: The Rule of the Last Antecedent

According to the last antecedent rule, if you add a modifier at the end of a list, this modifier only applies to the last item mentioned on that list.

For example:

"Trucks, motorbikes, and cars in New York." If we interpret this sentence literally, it refers to trucks and motorbikes from non-specific cities or regions. The only vehicles from New York we are referring to are the cars. This is extremely tricky because, in most written and spoken English, the communicator and the audience know that the trucks are from NY, the motorbikes from NY, and the cars from NY. It's implied in the sentence.

Lockhart v. U.S.

"The question presented: how to interpret statutory mandatory minimum sentences for sexual abuse. The result: a 6-2 split, broadly extending the statute's reach. The cause: a dangling modifier . . . ."

According to the statute, a ten-year mandatory minimum sentence should be applied to anyone with a prior conviction, who is then convicted of first-degree sexual abuse "relating to aggravated sexual abuse, sexual abuse, or abusive sexual conduct involving a minor or ward." https://www.lexisnexis.com/commu nity/casebrief/p/casebrief-lockhart-v-united-states

According to the last antecedent rule, and most justices, the dangling modifier, 'involving a minor or ward,' could only be applied to abusive sexual conduct and not to the other offenses listed. In aggravated sexual abuse and sexual abuse cases, the victim didn't necessarily have to be underage to apply the ten-year mandatory minimum sentence.

The defendant, Avondale Lockhart, was caught in possession of child pornography and pleaded guilty. Mr. Lockhart had a prior conviction for sexual abuse of his adult girlfriend. This previous abuse of his adult girlfriend triggered the ten-year minimum sentence.

https://www.findlaw.com/legalblogs/supreme-court/the-supreme-court-comes-to-the-defense-of-the-dangling-modifier/

As stated above, we need to include any modifiers as closely as we can to the words they describe. Misplacing modifiers can lead to major misunderstandings and ambiguity. We often have to be extra-careful with one-word modifiers that limit the meaning of other words, like simply, exclusively, only, just, even, barely, nearly, or almost.

Exercise

What is the difference in meaning between these two sentences?

Option 1:

*Power issues **almost** led to 200 trains having to be canceled nationwide yesterday.*

Option 2:

*Power issues led to **almost** 200 trains having to be canceled nationwide yesterday.*

Answer:

Option 1:

Power issues almost led to 200 trains having to be canceled nationwide yesterday.

Meaning: The cancelations were narrowly avoided. The exact number of trains was 200.

Option 2:

Power issues led to almost 200 trains having to be canceled nationwide yesterday.

Meaning: The cancelations were not avoided, and almost 200 trains were canceled. It wasn't exactly 200 trains, the number was slightly lower, but we don't know exactly how many from the sentence.

Adding Descriptive Information with -ing phrases

We need to be careful not to complicate and distort our message when we add extra information using -ing verbs.

Exercise

Which sentence is clearer in meaning and easier to read? Why?

Option 1:

Sitting outside the courthouse, the client was updated on the current situation by the barrister.

Meaning: ------------------------------------

Option 2:

Sitting outside the courthouse, the barrister updated his client on the current situation.

Meaning: -------------------------------------

Answers:

Option 1:

Sitting outside the courthouse, the client was updated on the current situation by the barrister.

Meaning: Who was sitting outside the courthouse? The client? The barrister? Both? We don't know because it's not clear.

Option 2:

Sitting outside the courthouse, the barrister updated his client on the current situation.

Meaning: We know for certain that the barrister was outside the courthouse here. The client may have been there physically too or may have been on the phone, but the sentence is clear and organized. It conveys as much meaning as possible with fewer words.

Legal Terms Glossary

https://www.businessballs.com/legal-and-procurement/contracts-and-agreements-legal-terms-and-definitions-glossary/

425 Legal Documents and Templates

Here, you will find a downloadable MS Word booklet with the 425 legal documents and templates which you can use or edit as you please.

There is absolutely no need to sign up for our free resource newsletter, but if you do wish to receive more free resources =, including free books and templates, please do not hesitate to sign up!

I hope you have found this book useful. Thank you for reading.

www.idmbusinessenglish.com/thanks-again

About the Author

MARC ROCHE is originally from Manchester. Marc is a business communication coach, legal English trainer, writer, and exam preparation specialist. He has collaborated with organizations such as the British Council, the Royal Melbourne Institute of Technology and University of Technology Sydney among others. Marc has also worked with multinationals such as Nike, GlaxoSmithKline or Bolsas y Mercados. In his free time, he likes to travel, cook, write, play sports, watch football (Manchester City and Real Madrid) and spend time with friends and family.

Learn more about Marc at amazon.com/author/marcroche

Make sure to look the free training resources

for students and teachers at

www.idmbusinessenglish.com/free-templates

www.ingramcontent.com/pod-product-compliance
Lightning Source LLC
Chambersburg PA
CBHW021406210526
45463CB00001B/240